CW01650977

Cath Davies

KISSING LIFE ON THE LIPS

Poems

JP PUBLISHING

To Julia,
with much love,
Cath
xx

Original title: KISSING LIFE ON THE LIPS
Author: Cath Davies © 2020
© 2020 JP PUBLISHING
josephpauleditions@gmail.com
Printed in Spain
Cover design: JP PUBLISHING
1st edition
ISBN: 978-1-913914-02-8

Contents

To Darrell

Echoes

She spoke in her own voice.

For a minute, I swore
I could hear her mother talking.
Her grandmother.

Her great grandmother.
All the way back, all speaking
in her own voice.

Always, I can hear love, love.
For the telling of stories.
But for one, roaring female sound.

A scream from history.
A deafening echo
of all the women unreported.

It was then she sang.
For if they will not listen to your words,
then give them pitch.

She did and I was amazed.
I last heard her,
leading a revolution in song,

the chorus of her ancestors,
echoing, echoing.

Tree

I used to love naturally.
As a poet, I would have said,

I love you,

like the strong branches of an oak to my leaves.
Like the wind sifting,
the woods straining to the sky.

But times have changed.

Now I love digitally.
As a poet, I now say, I love you
in a text message falling through cyberspace.
In a data tree of branches,
an inbox of half-digested seeds.

And whereas before, you were my roots,
the trunk, the sapling where
I go to to grow,
now you are a language in binary code,
a digital forest I am lost in,

where love is a binary word.

Minutes

We all just wanna be loved in this life,
like the red trees in Autumn,
the drifting mists of Spring,
the high sun in Summer.

We don't want the piercing frost of Winter,
that is still beautiful no matter what.
We all just wanna be loved,
like a child testing snow for the first time,
like an old man smiling at misfortune,
like a young girl opening an umbrella at the rain.

We all just wanna be loved in this life,
for it is shorter than a minute on a bedside clock,
shorter than an hour in a distant galaxy,
shorter than all the years it took the light to get back.

Platonic

I sit, stitching, surrounded
by yarns,
needles and threads.

On my finger, a thimble,
on my brow,
beads of sweat.

Stitching, stitching,
our platonic worlds colliding.
You a man,
I a woman, but no more than that.

Mend this, you say,
and you hand me your heart.
I sigh, the hole is bigger than ever.
Quite rented apart.

So I sit, stitching, surrounded,
ever the sewing bee.
These seamstresses you place such faith in?
They can't darn like me.

Vegas

Sin City, you made us virtuous, baby.
Me, a bride,
wobbly in a red dress.

He, a whisky'd groom,
in a hired suit.

You rocked us, baby.
At the chapel, Downtown, the Strip.
Saw two sinners

holy happy.
Happy as pigs in shit.

Kissing Life On The Lips

If I'm still alive at forty five,
then I do know this.

If life gives you trouble,
then kiss it on the lips.

Snog the face off adversity,
be a world weary tart.

Do a striptease at misfortune,
and do it from the heart.

Take each set back by the shoulders,
and look it in the eyes.

Shout sweet nothings in its ears,
for it's a lover in disguise.

Jump into bed with disaster,
and lie there in its arms.

Roll the damn thing over,
and shower it with charm.

Above all, be totally fearless,
make a first date of every day.

Kiss life completely on the lips,
and go with it all the way.

The Art of Life

There is an art to life,
And we go through many phases.
The figurative nature
Of childhood,
Where we try to draw things
As they appear.
The cubism of adolescence,
Where faces distort
And make no sense.
The abstract expressionism
Of our twenties,
Where we throw paint at walls,
Wanting the bigger picture to be right.
Then the impressionism
Of relationships,
Where we see things
In different lights.

Then the pop art of children,
In primary colours and cartoons.
And the minimalism
Of work, where every dot and line
Is held to account.
I know not of a phase
That doesn't have a school.
The sculpture of age,
Where everyone respects
The shape you have carved for yourself.
Finally, the still life,
And a gallery of that life.
But never regret a brushstroke
In the one masterpiece
You will ever paint.
Your self-portrait, your nude,
Your priceless original.

No Regrets

She grew a garden of regrets.

Ivy wound its way
around her trellis of mistakes.

A compost of wrong directions
fermented the soil.

Snowdrops. Weeds.
They were indistinguishable.
She rolled up her sleeves,

planted pots of dreams
amid a bed of indecision and drama.

And her garden grew.
The skies rained on her regrets,

everywhere festooned.

But he had green fingers.

Hacking and clearing, he took roses
and made them real.
He nurtured rhododendrons,

and pulled the weeds
until she couldn't feel them anymore.

He honoured the sun.
Turned the soil until all was done.

And her regrets withered.
In a great withering, they went.

And the ivy wound its way again,
the world dreaming, dreaming.

Dandelions

And so they grew,
like stars pinching the grass.

Fingers of breeze
rummaged in the boxed garden,
pulling at the soil,

frenzied.
And the house stood,
empty but full of a furniture of secrets.

Like a music box,
a key in the lock would open it again,
and you, the figurine.

But I kept it closed.
Inside, violence spun you. Faster.

A storm of high-pitched voices at midnight,

and us, the neighbours.
We called the police, to protect your child.
Like red ink, blood specs

made headlines in the paper.
A yellow dandelion
trampled, a gossamer clock strangled

by the fingers of your ex.
But I do believe you are safe now.
Desperate, drugged,

he will not find it.
For I buried the key in the fertile earth,
where dandelions entwine it.

You Never Know

You never know
when the sun will wake
when the poem will come to you
when the day will break
You never know
if the money will last
if the Earth can support you
if the die is cast
You never know
any of these things
anything about tomorrow
anything it brings
So love until you're breathless
breathe the blue air
and thank what you believe in
thank just being here

Your Time Will Tell

Your time will tell
of your corporeal place,

your finite line
in an infinite space.

Your time will tell
how you try to rebound

the stars' great silence,
yet greater sound.

Your time will tell
of your mind, unspoken,

commenting to itself,
your words its token.

Your time will tell
how amid infinite choice,

you steered by instinct,
those stars a voice.

And if, at the end,
another time begins,

the stars reclaim you,
as is the nature of things.

Bed

But for a poem, and you,
naked in bed
and speaking through
naked verse as the earth moves.

Relativity

In space and time
there exists
our co-ordinate.

My heart starts
at that spot.
The bending of gravity

towards you.
The flow of time
suspended.

Relativity
is the Universe
matching

your position to mine.

The odds
are phenomenal.

I watch the stars
and wonder
how it happened.

Car

I saw a car
like
the one you
used to drive.

A Ford.
Beige as the moon
on a warm
night.

My eye
followed it
out
of sight,
also seeing
you,

as the man
you were
when you last drove
this car,

and just
as
I saw this car,
I will never
see
you as you
were
again.

#climatestrikes

This is a call to poetry.
Words are arms,
and there is no time left.

Jaws

Great white man,
his prey, America.

Whispers in the water.

Glutinous fish.
Bloated swim bladder.

Gills sliced like wounds,
he winds his way
through ink black depths.

Cult-like, they follow him.
Great ocean. Hubris.

He hones in on prey,
whipping up shoals

in a tidal wave of opinion.

He attacks. A predator,
unevolved for millennia
in a blood red sea.

Nemesis. The rip tides
and lethal currents,
the cataclysm, the tsunami,

sink great white man,
the jaws of America.

Shot At Dawn

The Private stands
at a post,
the guns pointing at him.

Commentary is useless.
The birds fly
as the guns fire.

His body falls.
Truth is the only desertion.

As his blood runs,
only the words of History
say cowardice.

They drop the guns.
Eyes do not see in front of them

the reality of PTSD.

The shellshock.
The hell of the slightest noise
in flashback.

And the War goes on.
100 years will pass before
the Private
stands trial again.

But this time,
we will catch the bullets.

This time,
we will only ask
what birdsong cries at him.

Jump Off

Two men stand at a cliff edge.

One wants to remain.
One leave.

The man who wants to leave,
Is gone in minutes.
Without any warning whatsoever,

He has jumped.

The world gasps.
Knows all is lost, and that the man
Will never return again.

Alas, cries everybody.

He jumped.

He bloody went and jumped!
And hell ensues.
It is an emergency,
And no one knows what to do.

Then the man who wants to remain.

What about him?

He stands at the clifftop,
Staring, at the choice the man made.
He cannot believe it.

He grieves for it.

As the other man free falls,
He pinches himself again and again.
But he is awake.

So the two men divide at the cliff edge.
As the world watches,
One remains,
And one leaves.

And there is anger,
And there is fear,
And there are accusations,
And there are lies.

And seconds later,
The falling man lands.
He lies motionless for a minute,

Then he stands.

The world erupts.
This isn't supposed to happen.

People just don't survive
100 foot drops.

From the cliff top,
The other man is interviewed.
'What did you see?'
They ask.

'Did you see anything?'

He cannot reply.

After all, how can you tell the media
You saw Unity,
In the form of an angel,
Give the falling man wings?

Angel In The Cold

Angel, singing into the cold.
Who betrayed you?
What atrocities run through your tears?
Cross-legged. Homeless.
Summer top spotted with rain.
Sleeping bag crumpled like a broken heart.
If I had a five pound note
I would not walk past,
guilt-stricken.
But all I have is an apology,
from my own purse, which is empty.
For my government's conscience; empty.
For a ghastly Austerity
that will shame an age.
Angel, your shock of vulnerability
shames me too.
There is a world

where I sit down and become you.
And you stand and become me.
For only luck is the difference.
Only justice can see you
walk away from me, my heart broken.
Angel in the cold.

Stolen Dreams

Violate my things, violate me.
I touch a vanished life,
and realise the world I longed to live in
has dissolved around me.
Vulnerability.
In a locked house,
I finger a lost necklace.
My husband has ghosts of watches
around his wrists.
They raped our privacy,
but revealed more of them than us.
They savaged our security,
but a strange courage comes at times like this.
Love is a bolt against the fear.
A kiss, a lock.
Addicted to things,
I replace a laptop, but only so I can write

words to defend me.
Vulnerability.
Energies still permeate the walls.
But I will take from this,
as somebody else, somewhere,
touches a vanished world,
they violate them, they violate all of us,
in a frantic vortex
with its stolen dreams of power.

Coup

It started with a grey morning.
Ash rain
fell from the sky.

For an August day,
it was cool.

By noon,
the clouds had cleared.
But the mood

was strange.
People huddled to talk
about the weather. It's all we do.

Teatime.
and everything had changed.

People were no longer

talking about the weather.
Ash grey rain
concerned nobody.

It was all about the prorogue.
But when I looked,
there were no floods. No rain.

Unless you count floods of people.
A rain of protest
at the ultimate betrayal.

A Bitter Pill

You're like a cog.
A pair of legs walking a tightrope
called society
strung between two poles.

Birth and death.

This is a cruel circus.
The Ringmasters
have destroyed the safety net.
It's full of holes.

The audience is in uproar
at the cruelty.
The caging of lions.
The tears of an elephant.

This is pure blood sport.

A bitter pill.
But your vote is your parachute out.
Your collective voice
can dismantle the tent.

End this circus.
Close this arena of clowns.

Angel

In the late hours
how language
falls apart in the mind.

At forty five
I am still fragmented.
History instructs
but does not repeat like people say.

An angel is clarity.
Dreaming,
I sleepwalk with the world
into a changed future.

Everywhere, dark forces march.
It seems no one
saw the angel

place a feather like a kiss
over torn lives.

But no matter.
I ask her to sing to me,
so that I may raise my head
above demons.
Catch with my hands the falling lies
thrown at us all.

But the personal is political.
Only in the late hours
do I feel yesterday's world vanish.
As dark forces march,
I can still hear her singing.

Each note tells us to face the pain.
Not harden
it into prejudice.

Jaguar

Darkness falls over a habitat.
As the sun retreats, green light coats the rainforest,
and glowing on a branch,
the parrot splays its feathers to court its mate.

Deep in the water,
in the dim, algae rich, mud bottomed river,
the crocodile, knarled and squat,
cuts to the surface to begin its hunt.

It is the simplest dance. The noisiest silence.
With their wings of carbon,
and lungs of oxygen, the birds fly headlong,
released into a wind of danger.

For Mother Nature is departing.
Between the falling trees, where a primate swings,

the heat increases by degree,
and the leaves become audible, deafening.

Meanwhile, in the White House sits a man
who says it is not happening . . .
Bring him here, where the warming has already begun,
and the jaguar cries to him in hunger.

You Must Want To Be Arrested

The Earth has no voice,
but for the talk of the trees, the shout
of mountains, the scream
of birds and the whispers of fish.

The Earth has no voice,
which may be why they do not listen.
Politicians, throw your agendas
into the raging fire, for you will not have a planet

to be deaf to if you do not.
The Earth has no voice,
but for Us, complicated homo sapiens
who have a universal language

that can speak amid the flames.
So speak. Shout this truth into their ears

until they listen; deafen them.
And run. Run through the streets,

the hills, the mountains, the skies;
douse the world with action.
Shout above the inferno, for the emergency
is here whether we hear it or not.

The Earth has no voice.
Speak for her. Speak to her. Save her,
for the smallest act, moves mountains later.
You must want to be arrested.

Inertia

Inertia is no longer required.
For it is winter,
and a warm wind
blows over the British Isles.

Look. For they wear t-shirts,
and balance ice-creams
in February. And our only Earth,
signals something is wrong.

If we are listening. If we are listening
then inertia is no longer required.
Look. How the polar bear,
balanced on the retreating ice,

signals for all our lives. Look,
how a generation misses school

to march on the streets.
For it is our young people now

who insist inertia is no longer required.
For they look, and it is winter,
and a warm wind
blows over the British Isles.

Floods In June

Rain falls.
Outside my window
streams a deadly summer.

In February, the heat came.
Opening the door,
I met Winter leaving.

I invited it in.
Kept it cold until April,
when the snow fell.

I am not alone.
The truth is that Winter
was my guest.

In June, it is knocking again.

But this time
I know that the Earth

is our host.
So I will step out.
Lead Winter into Summer
as the rain falls.

I will search for a Spring
I never saw,
in a catastrophe
called by the seasons.

Asleep At The Wheel

Today, the car
that is our Earth

crashed.
Early reports state
it was on

safari.
Amur Leopards, Gorillas,
Tigers,
were all lost.

Speculation is
mounting
that the driver,

a composite

of conflicting reports
that may

conclude
Man,
was asleep

at the wheel,
dreaming of stars,

while the world burns.

Greta Thunberg Is A Climate Activist

Life is a party,
a raucous, wild party.
But now and then,
the mind escapes.
You find yourself outside.
Drunk. Smoking.
Ashamed of all of it,
until an odd reckoning
descends.
Belief is everything.
In yourself. In the party.
In the ability
of everyone to get us
out of this mess.

A Different Colour Sky

There is a different colour sky,
somewhere out there . . .

They say longing can go forward or back.

I can wish for the stars and the moon,
of last night.

Or wish for the rainbow,
opening up like a postcard from the future.

What will it say?

Simply, that you survived the storm
and the rain,

and the rich sun,
is waiting to pour its wealth onto your face . . .

ACKNOWLEDGEMENTS:

'Dandelion' shortlisted for the Creative Futures Literary Awards in 2018

'Echoes' published by the Dear Reader literary e-zine in 2019

'Platonic' published by the Nine Muses literary e-zine in 2019